The Es

GW01445281

Air Fryer

Cookbook

Easy Recipes for Delicious Homemade

Dishes, Low-Carb Breakfast, Lunch And

Dinner For Rapid Weight Loss

Emily Coen

Disclaimer Notice:

Please note the information contained within this document is for educational and entertainment purposes only. All effort has been executed to present accurate, up to date, and reliable, complete information. No warranties of any kind are declared or implied. Readers acknowledge that the author is not engaging in the rendering of legal, financial, medical or professional advice. The content within this book has been derived from various sources. Please consult a licensed professional before attempting any techniques outlined in this book.

By reading this document, the reader agrees that under no circumstances is the author responsible for any losses, direct or indirect, which are incurred as a result of the use of information contained within this document, including, but not limited to, — errors, omissions, or inaccuracies

Table Of Content

Introduction

Congratulations on purchasing your copy of *The Essential Air Fryer Cookbook: Easy Recipes for Delicious Homemade Dishes, Low-Carb Breakfast, Lunch And Dinner For Rapid Weight Loss*, and thank you for doing so.

I'm glad that you have chosen to take this opportunity to welcome the **Air Fryer Diet** into your life. I'm sure this book will help you find all the information and tools you need to better integrate the **Air Fryer Diet** plan with your habits.

Also, I thought I would share with you some delicious ideas and recipes for all tastes and for the best of your low carb diet, which I hope you will appreciate.

You will find hundreds of easy to realize ideas that will best suit your situation or your needs at the moment, with all the preparation time, amount of servings, and the list of all the nutritional values you'll need.

BREAKFAST

Sausage Frittata

Preparation Time: 15 minutes

Cooking time: 11 minutes

Servings: 2

Ingredients:

- ½ of chorizo sausage, sliced

- ½ cup frozen corn

- 1 large potato, boiled, peeled and cubed

- 3 jumbo eggs

- 2 tablespoons feta cheese, crumbled

- 1 tablespoon olive oil

- Salt and black pepper, to taste

Directions:

1. Preheat the Air fryer to 355 0 F and grease an Air Fryer pan.

2. Whisk together eggs with salt and black pepper in a bowl.

3. Heat olive oil in the Air Fryer pan and add sausage, corn and potato.

4. Cook for about 6 minutes and stir in the whisked eggs.

5. Top with cheese and cook for about 5 minutes.

Trout Frittata

Preparation Time: 15 minutes

Cooking time: 23 minutes

Servings: 4

Ingredients:

- 1 onion, sliced

- 6 eggs

- 2 hot-smoked trout fillets, chopped

- ¼ cup fresh dill, chopped

- 1 tomato, chopped

- 2 tablespoons olive oil

- ½ tablespoon horseradish sauce

- 2 tablespoons crème fraiche

Directions:

1. Preheat the Air fryer to 325 o F and grease a baking dish lightly.

2. Whisk together eggs with horseradish sauce and crème fraiche in a bowl.

3. Heat olive oil in a pan and add onions.

4. Sauté for about 3 minutes and transfer into a baking dish.

5. Stir in the whisked eggs, trout, tomato and dill.

6. Arrange the baking dish into an air fryer basket and cook for about 20 minutes.

7. Dish out and serve hot.

Nutrition:

Calories: 429, Fat: 38.1g, Carbohydrates: 5.5g, Sugar: 2.1g, Protein: 17.3g, Sodium: 252mg

Scrambled Eggs

Preparation Time: 20 minutes

Servings: 2

Ingredients:

- 4 large eggs.

- ½ cup shredded sharp Cheddar cheese.

- 2 tbsp. unsalted butter; melted.

Directions:

1. Crack eggs into 2-cup round baking dish and whisk. Place dish into the air fryer basket.

2. Adjust the temperature to 400 Degrees F and set the timer for 10 minutes

3. After 5 minutes, stir the eggs and add the butter and cheese. Let cook 3 more minutes and stir again

4. Allow eggs to finish cooking an additional 2 minutes or remove if they are to your desired liking. Use a fork to fluff. Serve warm.

Nutrition: Calories: 359; Protein: 19.5g; Fiber: 0.0g; Fat: 27.6g; Carbs: 1.1g

Spaghetti Squash Fritters

Preparation Time: 23 minutes

Servings: 4

Ingredients:

- 2 cups cooked spaghetti squash

- 2 stalks green onion, sliced

- 1 large egg.

- ¼ cup blanched finely ground almond flour.

- 2 tbsp. unsalted butter; softened.

- ½ tsp. garlic powder.

- 1 tsp. dried parsley.

Directions:

1. Remove excess moisture from the squash using a cheesecloth or kitchen towel.

2. Mix all ingredients in a large bowl. Form into four patties

3. Cut a piece of parchment to fit your air fryer basket. Place each patty on the parchment and place into the air fryer basket

4. Adjust the temperature to 400 Degrees F and set the timer for 8 minutes. Flip the patties halfway through the cooking time. Serve warm.

Nutrition: Calories: 131; Protein: 3.8g; Fiber: 2.0g; Fat: 10.1g; Carbs: 7.1g

Cheesy Sausage Balls

Preparation Time: 22 minutes

Servings: 16 balls

Ingredients:

- 1 lb. pork breakfast sausage

- 1 large egg.

- 1 oz. full-fat cream cheese; softened.

- ½ cup shredded Cheddar cheese

Directions:

1. Mix all ingredients in a large bowl. Form into sixteen, 1-inchballs. Place the balls into the air fryer basket.

2. Adjust the temperature to 400 Degrees F and set the timer for 12 minutes. Shake the basket two or three times during cooking

3. Sausage balls will be browned on the outside and have an internal temperature of at least 145 Degrees F when completely cooked.

Nutrition: Calories: 424; Protein: 22.8g; Fiber: 0.0g; Fat: 32.2g; Carbs: 1.6g

MAIN

White Beans with Rosemary

Preparation time: 10 minutes • Cooking time: 20 minutes • Servings: 10

INGREDIENTS

- 2pounds white beans, cooked
- 3celery stalks, chopped
- 2carrots, chopped
- 1bay leaf
- 1yellow onion, chopped
- 3garlic cloves, minced
- 1teaspoon rosemary, dried
- 1teaspoon oregano, dried
- 1teaspoon thyme, dried
- A drizzle of olive oil
- Salt and black pepper to the taste
- 28ounces canned tomatoes, chopped
- 6cups chard, chopped

DIRECTIONS

1. In your air fryer's pan, mix white beans with celery, carrots, bay leaf, onion, garlic, rosemary, oregano, thyme, oil, salt, pepper, tomatoes and chard, toss, cover and cook at 365 degrees F for 20 minutes.
2. Divide into bowls and serve.

3. Enjoy!

NUTRITION: Calories 341, Fat 8, Fiber 12, Carbs 20, Protein 6

Spinach and Lentils Mix

Preparation time: 10 minutes Cooking time: 15 minutes Servings: 8

INGREDIENTS

- 10 ounces spinach
- 2cups canned lentils, drained
- 1tablespoon garlic, minced
- 15ounces canned tomatoes, chopped
- 2cups cauliflower florets
- 1teaspoon ginger, grated
- 1yellow onion, chopped
- 2tablespoons curry paste
- ½ teaspoon cumin, ground
- ½ teaspoon coriander, ground
- 2teaspoons stevia
- A pinch of salt and black pepper
- ¼ cup cilantro, chopped
- 1tablespoon lime juice

DIRECTIONS

1. In a pan that fits your air fryer, mix spinach with

lentils, garlic, tomatoes, cauliflower, ginger, onion, curry paste, cumin, coriander, stevia, salt, pepper and lime juice, stir, introduce in the fryer and cook at 370 degrees F for 15 minutes.

2. Add cilantro, stir, divide into bowls and serve.

3. Enjoy!

NUTRITION: Calories 265, Fat 1, Fiber 7, Carbs12, Protein 7

Chipotle Green Beans

Preparation time: 10 minutes • Cooking time: 16 minutes • Servings: 6

INGREDIENTS

- 1yellow onion, chopped
- 1pound green beans, halved
- 2teaspoons cumin, ground
- A drizzle of olive oil
- 12ounces corn
- ¼ teaspoon chipotle powder
- 1cup salsa

DIRECTIONS

1. In a pan that fits your air fryer, combine oil with onion, green beans, cumin, corn, chipotle powder and salsa, toss, introduce in your air fryer and cook at 365 degrees F for 16 minutes.
2. Divide between plates and serve.
3. Enjoy!

NUTRITION: Calories 224, Fat 2, Fiber 12, Carbs 14, Protein 10

Tomato and Cranberry Beans Pasta

Preparation time: 10 minutes • Cooking time: 15 minutes • Servings: 8

INGREDIENTS

- 2cups canned cranberry beans, drained
- 2celery ribs, chopped
- 1yellow onion, chopped
- 7garlic cloves, minced
- 1teaspoon rosemary, chopped
- 26ounces canned tomatoes, chopped
- ¼ teaspoon red pepper flakes
- 2teaspoons oregano, dried
- 3teaspoons basil, dried
- ½ teaspoon smoked paprika
- A pinch of salt and black pepper
- 10ounces kale, roughly chopped
- 2cups whole wheat vegan pasta, cooked

DIRECTIONS

4. In a pan that fits your air fryer, combine beans with celery, onion, garlic, rosemary, tomatoes, pepper flakes, oregano, basil, paprika, salt, pepper and kale, introduce in your air fryer and cook at 365 degrees F for 15 minutes.

5. Divide vegan pasta between plates, add cranberry mix on top and serve.
6. Enjoy!

NUTRITION: Calories 251, Fat 2, Fiber 12, Carbs 12, Protein 6

Cajun Mushrooms with Veggies and Beans

Preparation time: 10 minutes • Cooking time: 15 minutes • Servings: 4

INGREDIENTS

- 3garlic cloves, minced 2 tablespoons olive oil
- 1green bell pepper, chopped
- 1yellow onion, chopped
- 2celery stalks, chopped
- 15ounces canned tomatoes, chopped
- 8ounces white mushrooms, sliced
- 15ounces canned kidney beans, drained
- 1zucchini, chopped
- 1tablespoon Cajun seasoning
- Salt and black pepper to the taste

DIRECTIONS

1. In your air fryer's pan, mix oil with bell pepper, onion, celery, garlic, tomatoes, mushrooms, beans, zucchini, Cajun seasoning, salt and pepper, stir, cover and cook on at 370 degrees F for 15 minutes.
2. Divide veggie mix between plates and serve.
3. Enjoy!

NUTRITION: Calories 312, Fat 4, Fiber 7, Carbs 19, Protein 4

Squash Bowls

Preparation time: 10 minutes • Cooking time: 20 minutes •
Servings: 5

INGREDIENTS

- 1big butternut squash, peeled and roughly
  cubed
- 2cups broccoli florets
- 1tablespoon sesame seeds
- For the salad dressing:
    - 1and ½ tablespoon stevia
    - 3tablespoons wine vinegar
    - 3tablespoons olive oil
    - 1tablespoon coconut aminos
    - 1tablespoon ginger, grated
    - 2garlic cloves, minced
    - 1teaspoon sesame oil

DIRECTIONS

1. In your blender, mix stevia with vinegar, oil, aminos, ginger, garlic and sesame oil, pulse really well and leave aside for now.
2. In your air fryer, mix squash with the dressing you've made, broccoli and sesame seeds, toss, cover and cook at 370 degrees F for 20 minutes.
3. Divide salad into bowls and serve.

4. Enjoy!

NUTRITION: Calories 250, Fat 4, Fiber 6, Carbs 26, Protein 6

SIDES

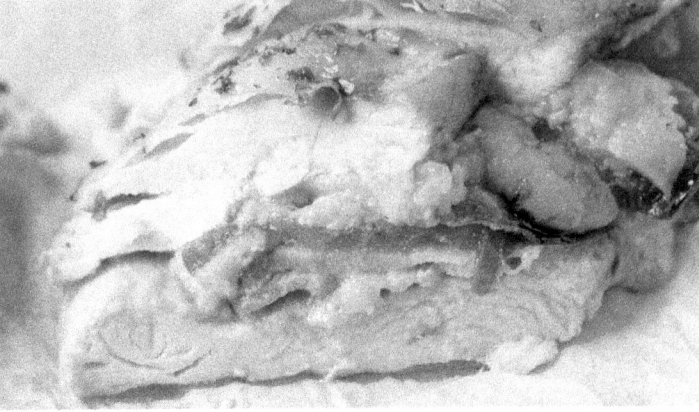

Endives and Rice Mix

Preparation time: 5 minutes Cooking time: 20 minutes Servings: 4

Ingredients:

• 2 scallions, chopped

• 3 garlic cloves, minced

• 1 tablespoon olive oil

• Salt and black pepper to taste

• . cup white rice

• 1 cup veggie stock

• 1 teaspoon chili sauce

• 4 endives, trimmed and shredded

Directions:

1. Take the oil and grease a pan that fits your air fryer.

2. Add all other ingredients and toss.

3. Place the pan in the air fryer and cookat 365 degrees F for 20 minutes.

4. Divide everything between plates and serve as a side dish.

Nutrition: calories 200, fat 7, fiber 4, carbs 9, protein 5

Turmeric Cabbage Mix

Preparation time: 5 minutes

Cooking time: 12 minutes

Servings: 4

Ingredients:

- 1 tablespoon olive oil

- 1 big green cabbage head, shredded

- ½ cup yellow onion, chopped

- 2 teaspoons turmeric powder

- Salt and black pepper to taste

- 4 tablespoons tomato sauce

Directions:

1. Take the oil and grease a pan that fits your air fryer.

2. Add all of the other ingredients and toss.

3. Place the pan in the fryer and cook at 365 degrees F for 12 minutes.

4. Divide between plates and serve as a side dish.

Nutrition: calories 188, fat 3, fiber 4, carbs 9, protein 7

Brown Lentils Mix

Preparation time: 10 minutes

Cooking time: 15 minutes

Servings: 4

Ingredients:

- 1 cup canned brown lentils, drained

- 1 teaspoon olive oil

- 2 tomatoes, chopped

- 4 garlic cloves, minced

- 1 teaspoon ginger, grated

- ½ teaspoon turmeric powder

- ¼ teaspoon cinnamon powder

- ¼ teaspoon cardamom powder

- Salt and black pepper to taste

- 8 ounces baby spinach

Directions:

1. In a pan that fits your air fryer, add all of the listed ingredients and toss.

2. Place the pan the fryer and cook at 370 degrees F for 15 minutes.

3. Divide the lentils between plates and serve as a side dish.

Nutrition: calories 188, fat 4, fiber 8, carbs 15, protein 7

Sweet Pepper Slices

Preparation Time: 20 minutes

Cooking time: 10 minutes

Servings: 2

Ingredients:

- 1 sweet red pepper

- 1 yellow sweet pepper

- 1 garlic clove

- 1 tablespoon apple cider vinegar

- 1 teaspoon olive oil

- ½ teaspoon dried dill

- ½ teaspoon dried parsley

- 1 teaspoon butter

- 1 pinch salt

Directions:

1. Wash the sweet peppers carefully and discard seeds.

2. Slice the sweet peppers.

3. Preheat the air fryer to 400 F.

4. Toss the butter in the air fryer basket and melt it.

5. Then add the sweet peppers slices.

6. Cook the sweet peppers for 10 minutes.

7. Shake them well after 5 minutes of cooking.

8. Meanwhile, peel the garlic clove and slice it.

9. Combine the sliced garlic with the apple cider vinegar and olive oil.

10. Add dried dill and dried parsley.

11. Sprinkle the mixture with the pinch of salt and whisk it well.

12. When the peppers are cooked – let the chill till the room temperature.

13. Then sprinkle the sweet peppers with the oily mixture well.

14. Put the meal in the fridge for 10 minutes.

15. Serve it!

Nutrition: calories 86, fat 4.6, fiber 1.7, carbs 11.1, protein 1.7

Indian Red Potatoes

Preparation time: 10 minutes

Cooking time: 20 minutes

Servings: 5

Ingredients:

- 2 pounds red potatoes, cubed

- ½ teaspoon mustard seeds

- 1 teaspoon garlic, minced

- ¼ cup veggie stock

- ½ cup mint

- ½ cup cilantro

- 1 teaspoon ginger, grated

- 2 teaspoons lime juice

- Salt and black pepper to taste

Directions:

1. In a blender, add the stock, mint, cilantro, ginger, lime juice, salt, and pepper; pulse well.

2. Then place this mint mix into a pan that fits your air fryer, along with the remaining ingredients, and toss.

3. Place the pan in the fryer and cook at 370 degrees F for 20 minutes.

4. Divide the potatoes between plates and serve as a side dish.

Nutrition: calories 199, fat 4, fiber 7, carbs 12, protein 6

SEAFOOD

Simple Salmon

Preparation Time: 5 minutes

Cooking time: 10 minutes

Servings: 2

Ingredients:

- 2, 6-ouncessalmon fillets

- Salt and black pepper, as required

- 1 tablespoon olive oil

Directions:

1. Preheat the Air fryer to 390 o F and grease an Air fryer basket.

2. Season each salmon fillet with salt and black pepper and drizzle with olive oil.

3. Arrange salmon fillets into the Air fryer basket and cook for about 10 minutes.

4. Remove from the Air fryer and dish out the salmon fillets onto the serving plates.

Nutrition:

Calories: 285, Fat: 17.5g, Carbohydrates: 0g, Sugar: 0g, Protein: 33g, Sodium: 153mg

Cajun Spiced Salmon

Preparation Time: 10 minutes

Cooking time: 8 minutes

Servings: 2

Ingredients:

- 2, 7-ounces>-¾-inch thicksalmon fillets

- 1 tablespoon Cajun seasoning

- ½ teaspoon sugar

- 1 tablespoon fresh lemon juice

Directions:

1. Preheat the Air fryer to 365 0 F and grease an Air fryer grill pan.

2. Season the salmon evenly with Cajun seasoning and sugar.

3. Arrange the salmon fillets into the Air fryer grill pan, skin-side up.

4. Cook for about 8 minutes and dish out the salmon fillets in the serving plates.

5. Drizzle with the lemon juice and serve hot.

Nutrition:

Calories: 268, Fats: 12.3g, Carbohydrates: 1.2g, Sugar: 1.2g, Proteins: 38.6g, Sodium: 164mg

Saucy Garam Masala Fish

Preparation Time: 25 minutes

Servings: 2

Nutrition: 301 Calories; 12.1g Fat; 2.3g Carbs; 43g Protein; 1.6g Sugars

Ingredients

☐ 2 teaspoons olive oil

☐ 1/4 cup coconut milk

☐ 1/2 teaspoon cayenne pepper

☐ 1 teaspoon Garam masala

☐ 1/4 teaspoon Kala namak, Indian black salt

☐ 1/2 teaspoon fresh ginger, grated

☐ 1 garlic clove, minced

☐ 2 catfish fillets

☐ 1/4 cup coriander, roughly chopped

Directions

1. Preheat your Air Fryer to 390 degrees F. Then, spritz the baking dish with a nonstick cooking spray.

2. In a mixing bowl, whisk the olive oil, milk, cayenne pepper, Garam masala, Kala namak, ginger, and garlic.

3. Coat the catfish fillets with the Garam masala mixture. Cook the catfish fillets in the preheated Air Fryer approximately 18 minutes, turning over halfway through the cooking time.

4. Garnish with fresh coriander and serve over hot noodles if desired.

1. Grilled Salmoon Steaks

Preparation Time: 45 minutes

Servings: 4

Nutrition: 420 Calories; 23g Fat; 2.5g Carbs; 48.5g Protein; 0.7g Sugars

Ingredients

- 2 cloves garlic, minced

- 4 tablespoons butter, melted

- Sea salt and ground black pepper, to taste

- 1 teaspoon smoked paprika

- 1/2 teaspoon onion powder

- 1 tablespoon lime juice

- 1/4 cup dry white wine

- 4 salmon steaks

Directions

1. Place all ingredients in a large ceramic dish. Cover and let it marinate for 30 minutes in the refrigerator.

2. Arrange the salmon steaks on the grill pan. Bake at 390 degrees for 5 minutes, or until the salmon steaks are easily flaked with a fork.

3. Flip the fish steaks, baste with the reserved marinade, and cook another 5 minutes. Bon appétit!

Easy Lobster Tails

Preparation Time: 20 minutes

Servings: 5

Nutrition: 422 Calories; 7.9g Fat; 49.9g Carbs; 35.4g Protein; 3.1g Sugars

Ingredients

- 2 pounds fresh lobster tails, cleaned and halved, in shells

- 2 tablespoons butter, melted

- 1 teaspoon onion powder

- 1 teaspoon cayenne pepper

- Salt and ground black pepper, to taste

- 2 garlic cloves, minced

- 1 cup cornmeal

- 1 cup green olives

Directions

1. In a plastic closeable bag, thoroughly combine all ingredients; shake to combine well.

2. Transfer the coated lobster tails to the greased cooking basket.

3. Cook in the preheated Air Fryer at 390 degrees for 6 to 7 minutes, shaking the basket halfway through. Work in batches.

4. Serve with green olives and enjoy!

Spicy Curried King Prawns

Preparation Time: 10 minutes

Servings: 2

Nutrition: 220 Calories; 9.7g Fat; 15.1g Carbs; 17.6g Protein; 2.2g Sugars

Ingredients

- 12 king prawns, rinsed

- ☐ 1 tablespoon coconut oil

- 1/2 teaspoon piri piri powder

- Salt and ground black pepper, to taste

- 1 teaspoon garlic paste

- 1 teaspoon onion powder

- 1/2 teaspoon cumin powder

- 1 teaspoon curry powder

Directions

1. In a mixing bowl, toss all ingredient until the prawns are well coated on all sides.

2. Cook in the preheated Air Fryer at 360 degrees F for 4 minutes. Shake the basket and cook for 4 minutes more.

3. Serve over hot rice if desired. Bon appétit!

POULTRY

Farmhouse Roast Turkey

Preparation Time: 50 minutes

Servings: 6

Nutrition: 316 Calories; 24.2g Fat; 2.5g Carbs; 20.4g Protein; 1.1g Sugars

Ingredients

- 2 pounds turkey

- 1 tablespoon fresh rosemary, chopped

- 1 teaspoon sea salt

- 1/2 teaspoon ground black pepper

- 1 onion, chopped

- 1 celery stalk, chopped

Directions

1. Start by preheating your Air Fryer to 360 degrees F. Spritz the sides and bottom of the cooking basket with a nonstick cooking spray.

2. Place the turkey in the cooking basket. Add the rosemary, salt, and black pepper. Cook for 30 minutes in the preheated Air Fryer.

3. Add the onion and celery and cook an additional 15 minutes. Bon appétit!

Bacon Wrapped Chicken Breasts

Servings: 4

Preparation Time: 20 minutes

Cooking Time: 23 minutes

Ingredients

- 1 tablespoon palm sugar

- 6-7 Fresh basil leaves

- 2 tablespoons fish sauce

- 2 tablespoons water

- 2, 8-ounceschicken breasts, cut each breast in half horizontally

- Salt and ground black pepper, as required

- 12 bacon strips

- 1½ teaspoon honey

Instructions

1. In a small heavy-bottomed pan, add palm sugar over medium-low heat and cook for about 2-3 minutes or until caramelized, stirring continuously.

2. Add the basil, fish sauce and water and stir to combine.

3. Remove from heat and transfer the sugar mixture into a large bowl.

4. Sprinkle each chicken breast with salt and black pepper.

5. Add the chicken pieces in sugar mixture and coat generously.

6. Refrigerate to marinate for about 4-6 hours.

7. Set the temperature of Air Fryer to 365 degrees F. Grease an Air Fryer basket.

8. Wrap each chicken piece with 3 bacon strips.

9. Coat each piece slightly with honey.

10. Arrange chicken pieces into the prepared Air Fryer basket.

11. Air Fry for about 20 minutes, flipping once halfway through.

12. Remove from Air Fryer and transfer the chicken pieces onto a serving platter.

13. Serve hot.

Nutrition:

Calories: 365

Carbohydrate: 2.7g

Protein: 30.2g

Fat: 24.8g

Sugar: 2.1g

Sodium: 1300mg

Buffalo Chicken Tenders

Servings: 3

Preparation Time: 20 minutes

Cooking Time: 12 minutes

Ingredients

- 1 tablespoon water

- 1 large egg

- 16 ounces boneless, skinless chicken breasts, sliced into tenders

- ½ cup pork rinds, crushed

- ½ cup unflavored whey protein powder

- ½ teaspoon garlic powder

- Salt and ground black pepper, as required

- 2 tablespoons butter, melted

- ¼ cup buffalo wing sauce

Instructions

1. In a large bowl, add the water, and egg. Beat until well combined.

2. Add the chicken and generously coat with egg mixture.

3. Place the chicken in a colander to drain completely.

4. In a shallow bowl, mix together the pork rinds, protein powder, garlic powder, salt, and black pepper.

5. Coat chicken tenders with the pork rinds mixture.

6. Set the temperature of Air Fryer to 400 degrees F. Grease an Air Fryer basket.

7. Arrange chicken tenders into the prepared Air Fryer basket and drizzle with the melted butter.

8. Air Fry for about 10-12 minutes.

9. Remove from Air Fryer and transfer the chicken tenders into a bowl.

10. Place with the buffalo sauce and toss to coat well.

11. Serve immediately.

Nutrition:

Calories: 292

Carbohydrate: 0.9g

Protein: 43.6g

Fat: 12.9g

Sugar: 0.2g

Sodium: 261mg

Loaded Chicken Burgers

Preparation Time: 30 minutes

Servings: 5

Nutrition: 476 Calories; 25.9g Fat; 29.9g

Carbs; 31.7g Protein; 2.5g Sugars

Ingredients

- 2 tablespoons olive oil

- 1 onion, finely chopped

- 2 green garlic, chopped

- 6 ounces mushrooms, chopped

- 1 ½ pounds ground chicken

- 1/3 cup parmesan cheese

- 1/4 cup pork rinds, crushed

- 1 tablespoon fish sauce

- 1 tablespoon tamari sauce

- 1 teaspoon Dijon mustard

- 5 soft hamburger buns

- 5 lettuce leaves

Directions

1. Heat a nonstick skillet over medium-high heat; add olive oil. Once hot, sauté the onion until tender and translucent, about 3 minutes.

2. Add the garlic and mushrooms and cook an additional 2 minutes, stirring frequently.

3. Add the ground chicken, cheese, pork rind, fish sauce, and tamari sauce; mix until everything is well incorporated.

4. Form the mixture into 5 patties. Transfer the patties to the lightly greased cooking basket.

5. Cook in the preheated Air Fryer at 370 degrees F for 8 minutes; then, flip them over and cook for 8 minutes on the other side.

6. Serve on burger buns, garnished with mustard and lettuce. Bon appétit!

Breaded Chicken Tenderloins

Servings: 4

Preparation Time: 15 minutes

Cooking Time: 15 minutes

Ingredients

- 1 egg, beaten

- 2 tablespoons vegetable oil

- ½ cup breadcrumbs

- 8 skinless, boneless chicken tenderloins

Instructions

1. In a shallow dish, beat the egg.

2. In another dish, add the oil and breadcrumbs and mix until a crumbly mixture forms.

3. Dip the chicken tenderloins into beaten egg and then coat with the breadcrumbs mixture.

4. Shake off the excess coating.

5. Set the temperature of Air Fryer to 355 degrees F. Grease an Air Fryer basket.

6. Arrange chicken tenderloins into the prepared Air Fryer basket in a single layer.

7. Air Fry for about 12-15 minutes.

8. Remove from Air Fryer and transfer the chicken thighs onto a serving platter.

9. Serve hot.

Nutrition:

Calories: 271

Carbohydrate: 12g

Protein: 30.4g

Fat: 11.5g

Sugar: 0.9g

Sodium: 113mg

Chicken with Golden Roasted Cauliflower

Preparation Time: 30 minutes

Servings: 4

Nutrition: 388 Calories; 18.9g Fat; 5.6g Carbs; 47.3g Protein; 1.3g Sugars

Ingredients

- 2 pounds chicken legs

- 2 tablespoons olive oil

- 1 teaspoon sea salt

- 1/2 teaspoon ground black pepper

- 1 teaspoon smoked paprika

- 1 teaspoon dried marjoram

- 1, 1-poundhead cauliflower, broken into small florets

- 2 garlic cloves, minced

- 1/3 cup Pecorino Romano cheese, freshly grated

- 1/2 teaspoon dried thyme

- Salt, to taste

Directions

1. Toss the chicken legs with the olive oil, salt, black pepper, paprika, and marjoram.

2. Cook in the preheated Air Fryer at 380 degrees F for 11 minutes. Flip the chicken legs and cook for a further 5 minutes.

3. Toss the cauliflower florets with garlic, cheese, thyme, and salt.

4. Increase the temperature to 400 degrees F; add the cauliflower florets and cook for 12 more minutes. Serve warm.

MEAT

Beef and Balsamic Marinade

Preparation Time: 40 minutes Servings: 4

Ingredients:

• 4 medium beef steaks

• 3 garlic cloves; minced

• 1 cup balsamic vinegar

• 2 tbsp. olive oil

• Salt and black pepper to taste.

Directions:

1. Take a bowl and mix steaks with the rest of the ingredients and toss.

2. Transfer the steaks to your air fryer's basket and cook at 390°F for 35 minutes, flipping them halfway

3. Divide between plates and serve with a side salad.

Nutrition: Calories: 273; Fat: 14g; Fiber:

4g; Carbs: 6g; Protein: 19g

Pulled Pork

Preparation Time: 2 hours

Servings: 8

Ingredients:

- 1, 4-poundpork shoulder

- ☐ 2 tbsp. chili powder

- ½ tsp. ground black pepper

- ½ tsp. cumin

- ½ tsp. onion powder.

- 1 tsp. garlic powder.

Directions:

1. In a small bowl, mix chili powder, garlic powder, onion powder, pepper and cumin. Rub the spice mixture over the pork shoulder, patting it into the skin

2. Place pork shoulder into the air fryer basket. Adjust the temperature to 350 Degrees F and set the timer for 150 minutes.

3. Pork skin will be crispy and meat easily shredded with two forks when done. The internal temperature should be at least 145 Degrees F

Nutrition: Calories: 537; Protein: 42.6g; Fiber: 0.8g; Fat: 35.5g; Carbs: 1.5g

Lamb and Pine Nuts Meatballs

Preparation Time: 35 minutes

Servings: 4

Ingredients:

- 1 ½ lb. lamb, ground

- 2 garlic cloves; minced

- 1 egg, whisked

- 1 scallion; chopped

- ½ cup pine nuts, toasted and chopped.

- 1 tbsp. olive oil

- 1 tbsp. thyme; chopped

- A pinch of salt and black pepper

Directions:

1. Take a bowl and mix the lamb with the rest of the ingredients except the oil, stir well and shape medium meatballs out of this mix

2. Grease the meatballs with the oil, put them in your air fryer's basket and cook at 380°F for 15 minutes on each side. Divide between plates and serve with a side salad

Nutrition: Calories: 287; Fat: 12g; Fiber: 3g; Carbs: 6g; Protein: 17g

Juicy Pork Chops

Preparation Time: 20 minutes

Servings: 2

Ingredients:

- 2, 4-oz.boneless pork chops

- 2 tbsp. unsalted butter, divided.

- ¼ tsp. ground black pepper

- ¼ tsp. dried oregano.

- 1 tsp. chili powder

- ½ tsp. cumin

- ½ tsp. garlic powder.

Directions:

1. In a small bowl, mix chili powder, garlic powder, cumin, pepper and oregano. Rub dry rub onto pork chops. Place pork chops into the air fryer basket. Adjust the temperature to 400 Degrees F and set the timer for 15 minutes

2. The internal temperature should be at least 145 Degrees F when fully cooked. Serve warm, each topped with 1 tbsp. butter.

Nutrition: Calories: 313; Protein: 24.4g; Fiber: 0.7g; Fat: 22.6g; Carbs: 1.8g

BBQ Meaotballs

Preparation Time: 24 minutes

Servings: 4

Ingredients:

- ¼ lb. ground Italian sausage

- 1 lb. 80/20 ground beef.

- 4 slices sugar-free bacon; cooked and chopped

- ¼ cup chopped white onion

- ¼ cup chopped pickled jalapeños.

- ½ cup low-carb, sugar-free barbecue sauce

- 1 large egg.

- 1 tsp. dried parsley.

- ¼ tsp. onion powder.

- ½ tsp. garlic powder.

Directions:

1. Take a large bowl, mix ground beef, sausage and egg until fully combined. Mix
in all remaining ingredients except barbecue sauce. Form into eight meatballs. Place meatballs into the air fryer basket.

2. Adjust the temperature to 400 Degrees F and set the timer for 14 minutes

3. Turn the meatballs halfway through the cooking time

---

4. When done, meatballs should be browned on the outside and have an internal temperature of at least 180 Degrees F. Remove meatballs from fryer and toss in barbecue sauce. Serve warm.

Nutrition: Calories: 336; Protein: 28.1g; Fiber: 0.4g; Fat: 19.5g; Carbs: 4.4g

Greek Lamb

Chops Preparation Time: 35 minutes Servings: 4

Ingredients:

• 4 lamb chops

• 1 cup Greek yogurt

• 2 tbsp. coconut oil; melted

• . tsp. turmeric powder

• 1 tsp. lemon zest, grated

• A pinch of salt and black pepper

Directions:

1. Take a bowl and mix the lamb chops with the rest of the ingredients and toss well.

2. Put the chops in your air fryer's basket and cook at 380°F for 15 minutes on each side

3. Divide between plates and serve

Nutrition: Calories: 283; Fat: 13g; Fiber: 3g;

Carbs: 6g; Protein: 15g

EGGS AND DAIRY

Scrambled Egg Muffins with Cheese

Preparation Time: 20 minutes Servings: 6

Nutrition: 234 Calories; 15.7g Fat; 5.3g Carbs;

17.6g Protein; 0.9g Sugars; 0.4g Fiber

Ingredients

• 6 ounces smoked turkey sausage, chopped

• 6 eggs, lightly beaten

• 2 tablespoons shallots, finely chopped

• 2 garlic cloves, minced

• Sea salt and ground black pepper, to taste

• 1 teaspoon cayenne pepper

• 6 ounces Monterey Jack cheese, shredded

Directions

1. Simply combine the sausage, eggs, shallots, garlic, salt, black pepper, and cayenne pepper in a mixing dish. Mix to combine well.

2. Spoon the mixture into 6 standardsize muffin cups with paper liners.

3. Bake in the preheated Air Fryer at 340 degrees F for 8 minutes. Top with the

cheese and bake an additional 8minutes. Enjoy!

VEGETABLES

Cabboage Sauté

Preparation time: 5 minutes Cooking time: 15 minutes Servings: 4

Ingredients:

• 1 pound red cabbage, shredded

• 1 tablespoon balsamic vinegar

• 2 red onions, sliced

• 1 tablespoon olive oil

• 1 tablespoon dill, chopped

• Salt and black pepper to the taste

Directions:

1. Heat up the air fryer with the oil at 380 degrees F, add the cabbage, onions and the other ingredients, toss and cook for 15 minutes.

2. Divide between plates and serve.

Nutrition: calories 100, fat 4, fiber 2, carbs 7, protein 2

Turmeric Carrots

Preparation time: 10 minutes Cooking time: 20 minutes Servings: 4

Ingredients:

• 1 pound baby carrots, peeled

• 3 tablespoons butter, melted

• 1 teaspoon turmeric powder

• 1 teaspoon rosemary, dried

• A pinch of salt and black pepper

• 1 tablespoon chives, chopped

Directions:

1. In your air fryer's basket, combine the carrots with the butter, turmeric and the other ingredients, toss and cook at 380 degrees F for 20 minutes.

2. Divide between plates and serve.

Nutrition: calories 90, fat 2, fiber 3, carbs 4, protein 4

Squash and Zucchini Mix

Preparation time: 10 minutes

Cooking time: 15 minutes

Servings: 4

Ingredients:

- 4 zucchinis, sliced

- 1 cup butternut squash, peeled and cubed

- 1 tablespoon olive oil

- 2 tablespoons lime juice

- Salt and black pepper to the taste

- 1 teaspoon oregano, dried

Directions:

1. In your air fryer, combine the zucchinis with the squash and the other ingredients, toss and cook at 380 degrees F for 15 minutes.

2. Divide the mix between plates and serve.

Nutrition: calories 125, fat 5, fiber 2, carbs 11, protein 5

Lemon Green Beans

Preparation time: 10 minutes

Cooking time: 10 minutes

Servings: 4

Ingredients:

- 1 pound green beans, trimmed and halved

- 1 tablespoon lemon zest, grated

- 2 garlic cloves, minced

- Juice of 1 lemon

- 1 tablespoon olive oil

- Salt and black pepper to the taste

Directions:

1. In your air fryer, combine the green beans with the lemon juice and the other ingredients, toss and cook at 400 degrees F for 10 minutes.

2. Divide the mix between plates and serve.

Nutrition: calories 181, fat 7, fiber 4, carbs 9, protein 3

Balsamic Squash

Preparation time: 10 minutes

Cooking time: 15 minutes

Servings: 4

Ingredients:

- 3 cups butternut squash, peeled and roughly cubed

- 2 tablespoons olive oil

- 1 tablespoon balsamic vinegar

- Salt and black pepper to the taste

- 2 teaspoons sweet paprika

- 1 teaspoon oregano, dried

Directions:

1. In your air fryer, combine the squash with the oil, vinegar and the other ingredients, toss and cook at 370 degrees F for 15 minutes.

2. Divide the mix between plates and serve.

Nutrition: calories 100, fat 1, fiber 3, carbs 8, protein 4

Olives and Potatoes

Preparation time: 10 minutes

Cooking time: 20 minutes

Servings: 4

Ingredients:

- 2 pounds potatoes, peeled and cubed

- 1 cup kalamata olives, pitted and halved

- 1 red onion, sliced

- 1 tablespoon lime juice

- 2 tablespoons olive oil

- Salt and black pepper to the taste

- 1 tablespoon hot paprika

Directions:

1. In your air fryer, combine the potatoes with the kalamata olives, onion and the other ingredients, toss and cook at 400 degrees F for 20 minutes.

2. Divide the mix between plates and serve..

Nutrition: calories 140, fat 3, fiber 4, carbs 10, protein 4

SNACKS

Crispy Crackling Bites

Preparation Time: 50 minutes

Servings: 10

Nutrition: 245 Calories; 14.1g Fat; 0g Carbs; 27.6g Protein; 0g Sugars; 0.5g Fiber

Ingredients

- 1 pound pork rind raw, scored by the butcher

- 1 tablespoon sea salt

- 2 tablespoons smoked paprika

Directions

1. Sprinkle and rub salt on the skin side of the pork rind. Allow it to sit for 30 minutes.

2. Roast at 380 degrees F for 8 minutes; turn them over and cook for a further 8 minutes or until blistered.

3. Sprinkle the smoked paprika all over the pork crackling and serve. Bon appétit!

Roasted Spicy Hot Dogs

Preparation Time: 20 minutes

Servings: 6

Nutrition: 542 Calories; 47.2g Fat; 5.7g Carbs; 21.1g Protein; 3.6g Sugars; 0.2g Fiber

Ingredients

- 6 hot dogs

- 1 tablespoon mustard

- 6 tablespoons ketchup, no sugar added

Directions

1. Place the hot dogs in the lightly greased Air Fryer basket.

2. Bake at 380 degrees F for 15 minutes, turning them over halfway through the cooking time to promote even cooking.

3. Serve on cocktail sticks with the mustard and ketchup. Enjoy!

Aromatic Kale Chips

Preparation Time: 5 minutes

Servings: 4

Nutrition: 91 Calories; 8.8g Fat; 3.2g Carbs; 1g Protein; 0g Sugars; 0.3g Fiber

Ingredients

- 2 ½ tablespoons olive oil

- 1 ½ teaspoons garlic powder

- 1 bunch of kale, torn into small pieces

- 2 tablespoons lemon juice

- 1 1/2 teaspoons seasoned salt

Directions

1. Toss your kale with the other ingredients.

2. Cook at 195 degrees F for 4 to 5 minutes, tossing kale halfway through.

3. Serve with your favorite dipping sauce.

BBQ Lil Smokies

Preparation Time: 20 minutes

Servings: 6

Nutrition: 275 Calories; 23.6g Fat; 3.6g Carbs; 11.9g Protein; 1.8g Sugars; 0.9g Fiber

Ingredients

- 1 pound beef cocktail wieners

- 10 ounces barbecue sauce, no sugar added

Directions

1. Start by preheating your Air Fryer to 380 degrees F.

2. Prick holes into your sausages using a fork and transfer them to the baking pan.

3. Cook for 13 minutes. Spoon the barbecue sauce into the pan and cook an additional 2 minutes.

4. Serve with toothpicks. Bon appétit!

Broccoli Fries with Spicy Dip

Preparation Time: 15 minutes

Servings: 4

Nutrition: 219 Calories; 19.3g Fat; 8.5g Carbs; 4.9g Protein; 2.8g Sugars; 2.5g Fiber

Ingredients

- 3/4 pound broccoli florets

- 1/2 teaspoon onion powder

- 1 teaspoon granulated garlic

- 1/2 teaspoon cayenne pepper

- Sea salt and ground black pepper, to taste

- 2 tablespoons sesame oil

- 4 tablespoons parmesan cheese, preferably freshly grated

Spicy Dip:

- 1/4 cup mayonnaise

- 1/4 cup Greek yogurt

- 1/4 teaspoon Dijon mustard

- 1 teaspoon hot sauce

Directions

1. Start by preheating the Air Fryer to 400 degrees F.

2. Blanch the broccoli in salted boiling water until al dente, about 3 to 4 minutes. Drain well and transfer to the lightly greased Air Fryer basket.

3. Add the onion powder, garlic, cayenne pepper, salt, black pepper, sesame oil, and parmesan cheese.

4. Cook for 6 minutes, tossing halfway through the cooking time.

5. Meanwhile, mix all of the spicy dip ingredients. Serve broccoli fries with chilled dipping sauce. Bon appétit!

Movie Night Zucchini Fries

Preparation Time: 26 minutes

Servings: 4

Nutrition: 135 Calories; 7.7g Fat; 8.2g Carbs; 9.2g Protein; 3.9g Sugars; 2.3g Fiber

Ingredients

- 2 zucchinis, slice into sticks

- 2 teaspoons shallot powder

- 1/4 teaspoon dried dill weed

- 2 teaspoons garlic powder - 1/2 cup Parmesan cheese, preferably freshly grated

- 1/3 teaspoon cayenne pepper

- 3 egg whites - 1/3 cup almond meal

- Cooking spray

- Salt and ground black pepper, to your liking

Directions

1. Pat the zucchini sticks dry using a kitchen towel.

2. Grab a mixing bowl and beat the egg whites until pale; then, add all the seasonings in the order listed above and beat again

3. Take another mixing bowl and mix together almond meal and the Parmesan cheese.

4. Then, coat the zucchini sticks with the seasoned egg mixture; then, roll them over the parmesan cheese mixture.

5. Lay the breaded zucchini sticks in a single layer on the tray that is coated lightly with cooking spray.

6. Bake at 375 degrees F for about 20 minutes until the sticks are golden brown. Serve with your favorite sauce for dipping.

Celery Chips with Harissa Mayonnaise Sauce

Preparation Time: 30 minutes

Servings: 3

Nutrition: 234 Calories; 23.7g Fat; 4.3g Carbs; 1.3g Protein; 1.9g Sugars; 1.5g Fiber

Ingredients

- 1/2 pound celery root

- 2 tablespoons olive oil

- Sea salt and ground black pepper, to taste

- Harissa Mayo

- 1/4 cup mayonnaise

- 2 tablespoons sour cream

- 1/2 tablespoon harissa paste

- ☐ 1/4 teaspoon ground cumin

- Salt, to taste

Directions

1. Cut the celery root into desired size and shape.

2. Then, preheat your Air Fryer to 400 degrees F. Now, spritz the Air Fryer basket with cooking spray.

3. Toss the celery chips with the olive oil, salt, and black pepper. Bake in the preheated Air Fryer for 25 to 30 minutes, turning them over every 10 minutes to promote even cooking.

4. Meanwhile, mix all ingredients for the harissa mayo. Place in your refrigerator until ready to serve. Bon appétit!

DESSERT

Chocolate Sauce

Preparation Time: 8 minutes

Cooking time: 4 minutes

Servings: 2

Ingredients:

- 3 tablespoon chocolate chips

- 2 tablespoon heavy cream

- 1 teaspoon butter

- 1 tablespoon milk

- ½ teaspoon vanilla extract

Directions:

1. Melt the butter and combine it with the heavy cream and milk.

2. Add vanilla extract and mix the mixture.

3. Preheat the air fryer to 400 F.

4. Put the chocolate chips in the air fryer basket and cook them for 2 minutes.

5. When the chocolate chips are melted – add the heavy cream mixture.

6. Cook the mixture for 2 minutes more.

7. After this, stir the mixture with the help of the spatula and cook it for 2 minutes more.

8. Stir it carefully until the sauce is homogenous.

9. Pour the sauce into the ramekins and serve. Enjoy!

Nutrition: calories 160, fat 12.3, fiber 0.5, carbs 10.3, protein 1.8

Oats Cookies

Preparation Time: 10 minutes

Cooking time: 9 minutes

Servings: 2

Ingredients:

- 3 tablespoon oatmeal flour

- 2 tablespoon sour cream

- 1 tablespoon brown sugar

- 1 teaspoon butter

- 1 pinch salt

- ½ teaspoon ground cardamom

- 1 egg

Directions:

1. Beat the egg in the bowl and whisk it.

2. Add the oatmeal flour and flour in the whisked egg.

3. After this, add sour cream, brown sugar, butter, salt, and ground cardamom.

4. Mix the mixture to get the homogenous dough.

5. Preheat the air fryer to 360 F.

6. Cover the air fryer basket with the parchment.

7. Make the medium cookies from the dough. Use the spoon for this step.

8. Place the cookies in the air fryer basket and cook for 9 minutes.

9. When the cookies are cooked – chill them well.

10. Taste and enjoy!

Nutrition: calories 115, fat 7, fiber 0.8, carbs 9.3, protein 4.2

Chocolate Yogurt Muffins

Servings: 9

Preparation Time: 15 minutes

Cooking Time: 10 minutes

Ingredients

- 1½ cups all-purpose flour

- ¼ cup sugar

- 2 teaspoons baking powder

- ½ teaspoon salt

- 1 cup yogurt

- 1/3 cup vegetable oil

- 1 egg

- 2 teaspoons vanilla extract

- ¼ cup mini chocolate chips

- ¼ cup pecans, chopped

Instructions

1. In a bowl, mix well flour, sugar, baking powder, and salt.

2. In another bowl, add the yogurt, oil, egg, and vanilla extract and whisk until well combined.

3. Add the flour mixture and mix until just combined.

4. Fold in the chocolate chips and pecans.

5. Set the temperature of air fryer to 355 degrees F. Grease 9 muffin molds.

6. Place mixture evenly into the prepared muffin molds.

7. Arrange the muffin molds into an air fryer basket.

8. Air fry for 10 minutes or until a toothpick inserted in the center comes out clean.

9. Remove the muffin molds from air fryer and place onto a wire rack to cool for about 10 minutes.

10. Finally, invert the muffins onto wire rack to completely cool before serving.

Nutrition

Calories: 246

Carbohydrate: 27.3g

Protein: 5g

Fat: 12.9g

Sugar: 10.2g

Sodium: 159mg

Brownies Muffins

Servings: 12

Preparation Time: 10 minutes

Cooking Time: 10 minutes

Ingredients

- 1 package Betty Crocker fudge brownie mix

- ¼ cup walnuts, chopped

- 1 egg

- 1/3 cup vegetable oil

- 2 teaspoons water

Instructions

1. In a bowl, mix well all the ingredients.

2. Set the temperature of air fryer to 300 degrees F. Grease 12 muffin molds.

3. Place mixture evenly into the prepared muffin molds.

4. Arrange the molds into an Air Fryer basket.

5. Air fry for 10 minutes or until a toothpick inserted in the center comes out clean.

6. Remove the muffin molds from air fryer and place onto a wire rack to cool for about 10 minutes.

7. Finally, invert the muffins onto wire rack to completely cool before serving.

Nutrition

Calories: 241

Carbohydrate: 36.9g

Protein: 2.8g

Fat: 9.6g

Sugar: 25g

Sodium: 155mg

Double Chocolate Muffins

Servings: 12

Preparation Time: 20 minutes

Cooking Time: 30 minutes

Ingredients

- 1 1/3 cups self-rising flour

- 2/3 cup plus 3 tablespoons caster sugar

- 2½ tablespoons cocoa powder

- 3½ ounces butter

- 5 tablespoons milk

- 2 medium eggs

- ½ teaspoon vanilla extract

- Water, as required

- 2½ ounces milk chocolate, finely chopped

Instructions

1. In a bowl, mix well flour, sugar, and cocoa powder.

2. With a pastry cutter, cut in the butter until a breadcrumb like mixture forms.

3. In another bowl, mix together the milk, and eggs.

4. Add the egg mixture into flour mixture and mix until well combined.

5. Add the vanilla extract and a little water and mix until well combined.

6. Fold in the chopped chocolate.

7. Set the temperature of air fryer to 355 degrees F. Grease 12 muffin molds.

8. Transfer mixture evenly into the prepared muffin molds.

9. Arrange the molds into an air fryer basket in 2 batches.

10. Air fry for about 9 minutes.

11. Now, set the temperature of air fryer to 320 degrees F.

12. Air fry for another 6 minutes or until a toothpick inserted in the center comes out clean.

13. Remove the muffin molds from air fryer and place onto a wire rack to cool for about 10 minutes.

14. Now, invert the muffins onto wire rack to cool completely before serving.

Nutrition

Calories: 207

Carbohydrate: 28.1g

Protein: 3.3g

Fat: 9.6g

Sugar: 16.5g

Sodium: 66mg

Fruity Oreo Muffins

Servings: 6

Preparation Time: 15 minutes

Cooking Time: 10 minutes

Ingredients

- 1 cup milk

- 1 pack Oreo biscuits, crushed

- 1 teaspoon cocoa powder

- ¼ teaspoon baking soda

- ½ teaspoon baking powder

- 1 banana, peeled and chopped

- 1 apple, peeled, cored and chopped

- 1 teaspoon honey

- 1 teaspoon fresh lemon juice

- A pinch of ground cinnamon

Instructions

1. In a bowl, add the milk, biscuits, cocoa powder, baking soda, and baking powder. Mix until a smooth mixture forms.

2. Set the temperature of air fryer to 320 degrees F. Grease 6 muffin cups.

3. Place mixture evenly into the prepared muffin cups.

4. Arrange the muffin cups into an air fryer basket.

5. Air fry for 10 minutes or until a toothpick inserted in the center comes out clean.

6. Remove from air fryer and place the muffin cups onto a wire rack to cool slightly.

7. Meanwhile, in another bowl, mix together the banana, apple, honey, lemon juice, and cinnamon.

8. Carefully, scoop some portion of muffins from the center to make a cup.

9. Fill each cup with fruit mixture.

10. Refrigerate to chill before serving.

Nutrition

Calories: 182

Carbohydrate: 31.4g

Protein: 3.1g

Fat: 5.9g

Sugar: 19.5g

Sodium: 196mg

Apple Pastries

Preparation Time: 15 minutes

Cooking time: 8 minutes

Servings: 2

Ingredients:

- 1 red apples

- 2 teaspoon brown sugar

- 1 teaspoon ground cinnamon

- 2 teaspoon butter

- 3 oz puff pastry

- 1 egg yolk

Directions:

1. Roll the puff pastry and cut it into 2 squares.

2. Roll the edges of the squares.

3. Then halve the apple and slice it.

4. Place the apple slices in the center of dough squares.

5. Then sprinkle the apples with the ground cinnamon, sugar, and butter.

6. Whisk the egg yolk and brush the dough edges.

7. Preheat the air fryer to 400 F.

8. Cover the air fryer basket with the parchment and put the pastries there.

9. Cook the dessert for 8 minutes or until it is cooked.

10. Serve the cooked dessert immediately.

11. Enjoy!

Nutrition: calories 367, fat 22.5, fiber 4, carbs 38.8, protein 4.8

Nut Cookies

Preparation Time: 15 minutes

Cooking time: 15 minutes

Servings: 2

Ingredients:

- 3 tablespoon flour

- 1 teaspoon butter

- 1 teaspoon cashew, crushed

- ½ teaspoon vanilla extract

- 1 tablespoon brown sugar

- ½ teaspoon cream

Directions:

1. Make the butter soft and place it in the big bowl.

2. Add flour and vanilla extract.

3. After this, add brown sugar and cream.

4. Knead the smooth and non-sticky dough.

5. Roll the dough and make the cookies with the help of the cutter.

6. Sprinkle every cookie with the crushed cashews.

7. Press the surface of the cookies lightly.

8. Preheat the air fryer to 360 F.

9. Put the cookies in the air fryer basket tray and cook the cookies for 15 minutes.

10. When the cookies are cooked – let them chill briefly.

11. Enjoy!

Nutrition: calories 88, fat 2.7, fiber 0.4, carbs 14, protein 1.5

Nutty Mix

Preparation Time: 5 minutes • Cooking Time: 4 minutes •
Servings: 6

NUTRITION:

- Calories: 316
- Fat: 29 g
- Carbs: 11.3 g
- Protein: 7.6 g
- Ingredients:
- 2cup mix nuts
- 1tsp. ground cumin
- 1tsp. chili powder
- 1tbsp. melted butter
- 1tsp. salt
- 1tsp. pepper

DIRECTIONS

1. Set all ingredients in a large bowl and toss until well coated.
2. Preheat the air fryer at 3500F for 5 minutes.
3. Add mix nuts in air fryer basket and air fry for 4 minutes. Shake basket halfway through.
4. Serve and enjoy.

Vanilla Spiced Soufflé

Preparation Time: 20 minutes • Cooking Time: 32 minutes •
Servings: 6

INGREDIENTS

- ¼ cup all-purpose flour
- 1cup whole milk
- 2tsps. vanilla extract
- 1tsp. cream of tartar
- 1vanilla bean
- 4egg yolks
- 1-oz. sugar
- ¼ cup softened butter
- ¼ cup sugar
- 5egg whites

DIRECTIONS

1. Combine flour and butter in a bowl until the mixture becomes a smooth paste.
2. Set the pan over medium flame to heat the milk. Add sugar and stir until dissolved.
3. Mix in the vanilla bean and bring to a boil.
4. Beat the mixture using a wire whisk as you add the butter and flour mixture.
5. Lower the heat to simmer until thick. Discard the vanilla bean. Turn off the heat.

6. Place them on an ice bath and allow to cool for 10 minutes.

7. Grease 6 ramekins with butter. Sprinkle each with a bit of sugar.

8. Beat the egg yolks in a bowl. Add the vanilla extract and milk mixture. Mix until combined.

9. Whisk together the tartar cream, egg whites, and sugar until it forms medium stiff peaks.

10. Gradually fold egg whites into the soufflé base. Transfer the mixture to the ramekins.

11. Put 3 ramekins in the cooking basket at a time. Cook for 16 minutes at 330 degrees. Move to a wire rack for cooling and cook the rest.

12. Sprinkle powdered sugar on top and drizzle with chocolate sauce before serving.

NUTRITION: Calories: 215   Fat: 12.2g   Carbs: 18.98g Protein: 6.66g

Apricot Blackberry Crumble

Preparation Time: 10 minutes • Cooking Time: 20 minutes • Servings: 8

INGREDIENTS

- 1cup flour
- 18oz. fresh apricots
- 5tbsps. cold butter
- ½ cup sugar
- 5½ oz. fresh blackberries
- Salt
- 2tbsps. lemon juice

DIRECTIONS

1. Put the apricots and blackberries in a bowl. Add lemon juice and 2 tbsps. of sugar. Mix until combined.
2. Transfer the mixture to a baking dish.
3. Put flour, the rest of the sugar, and a pinch of salt in a bowl. Mix well. Add a tbsp. of cold butter.
4. Combine the mixture until it becomes crumbly. Put this on top of the fruit mixture and press it down lightly.
5. Set the baking tray in the cooking basket.
6. Cook for 20 minutes at 390 degrees.

7. Allow to cool before slicing and serving.

NUTRITION: Calories: 217   Fat: 7.44g

Carbs: 36.2g Protein: 2.3g

Chocolate Cup cakes

Preparation Time: 5 minutes • Cooking Time: 12 minutes • Servings: 6

INGREDIENTS

- 3eggs
- ¼ cup caster sugar
- ¼ cup cocoa powder
- 1tsp. baking powder
- 1cup milk
- ¼ tsp. vanilla essence
- 2cup all-purpose flour
- 4tbsps. butter

DIRECTIONS

1. Preheat your Air Fryer to a temperature of 400°F (200°C).
2. Beat eggs with sugar in a bowl until creamy.
3. Add butter and beat again for 1-2 minutes.
4. Now add flour, cocoa powder, milk, baking powder, and vanilla essence, mix with a spatula.
5. Fill ¾ of muffin tins with the mixture and place

them into Air Fryer basket.

6. Let cook for 12 minutes.

7. Serve!

NUTRITION: Calories: 289 Protein: 8.72 g Fat: 11.5 g Carbs: 38.94 g

Chocolate Mayo Cake

Preparation Time: 15 minutes • Cooking Time: 2 minutes • Servings: 2

INGREDIENTS

- Large egg,
- Water, 2 tbsps.
- Swerve sugar substitute, 3 tbsps.
- Dark cocoa powder, 2 tbsps.
- Mayonnaise, ¼ cup
- Vanilla extract, ½ tsp.
- Cooking oil
- Baking powder, 1 tsp.
- Almond flour, 4 tbsps.
- Coconut flour, 1½ tbsps.

DIRECTIONS

1. Combine the dry ingredients in a 4-cup mixing bowl.
2. Whisk in the remaining ingredients to create a smooth batter.
3. Divide the batter into two 4-ounce ramekins, greased with cooking oil.
4. Place the ramekins in the air fryer basket and return the basket to the air fryer.
5. Cook them for 2 minutes on air fry mode at 3500 F.
6. Garnish with whipped cream.

7. Serve.

NUTRITION: Calories: 239   Fat: 17.1 g Carbs: 4.2 g

Protein: 6.9 g

Homemade French Fries

Preparation time: 30 minutes • Cooking time: 28 minutes • Servings: 4

INGREDIENTS

- 2reddish potatoes, cut into strips of 76 x 25 mm
- 1liter of cold water, to soak the potatoes
- 15ml of oil
- 3g garlic powder
- 2g of paprika
- Salt and pepper to taste
- Tomato sauce or ranch sauce, to serve

DIRECTION:

1. Cut the potatoes into 76 x 25 mm strips and soak them in water for 15 minutes.
2. Drain the potatoes, rinse with cold, dry water with paper towels.
3. Add oil and spices to the potatoes, until they are completely covered.
4. Preheat the air fryer, set it to 195°C.
5. Add the potatoes to the preheated air fryer. Set the timer to 28 minutes.
6. Be sure to shake the baskets in the middle of cooking.
7. Remove the baskets from the air fryer when you

have finished cooking and season the fries with salt and pepper.

8. Serve with tomato sauce or ranch sauce.

NUTRITION: Calories: 390 Fat: 36g Carbohydrates: 42g Protein: 5g Sugar: 4g Cholesterol: 0mg

Pumpkin Delights

Preparation Time: 20 minutes

Cooking time: 7 minutes

Servings: 2

Ingredients:

- ¼ teaspoon ground anise

- ¼ teaspoon vanilla extract

- 2 teaspoon honey

- ¼ teaspoon ground cinnamon

- ½ teaspoon ground ginger

- 1 teaspoon butter

- 10 oz pumpkin

Directions:

1. Peel the pumpkin and cut it into 4 pieces.

2. Combine together vanilla extract, ground anise, honey, ground cinnamon, ground ginger, and butter,

3. Churn the mixture. Preheat it if desired.

4. Then sprinkle the pumpkin pieces with the spice mixture and leave them for 15 minutes or till the pumpkin gives the juice.

5. Then preheat the air fryer to 400 F.

6. Put the pumpkin pieces in the air fryer basket.

7. Sprinkle the pumpkin pieces with the remaining juice mixture.

8. Cook the pumpkin pieces for 7 minutes.

9. Shake the pumpkin pieces after 3 minutes of cooking.

10. When the pumpkin pieces are cooked – they should be tender.

11. Let the cooked pumpkin pieces cool briefly.

12. Serve the dessert immediately or keep it in the fridge.

13. Enjoy!

Nutrition: calories 91, fat 2.4, fiber 4.4, carbs 18, protein 1.7

Blueberry Crumble

Preparation Time: 15 minutes

Cooking time: 15 minutes

Servings: 2

Ingredients:

- 3 tablespoon blueberry

- 1 tablespoon brown sugar

- 1 teaspoon lemon juice

- ¼ teaspoon ground nutmeg

- 2 tablespoon butter, soft

- 4 tablespoons flour

- ¼ teaspoon olive oil

- 2 teaspoon white sugar

Directions:

1. Mash the blueberries with the help of the fork.

2. Add lemon juice and brown sugar.

3. Mix the mixture up and add ground nutmeg.

4. Then combine together flour, soft butter, and white sugar.

5. Knead the soft dough.

6. Crumble the dough with the help of the fingertips.

7. Separate the crumbled dough into 2 parts.

8. Then cover the cake tin with the parchment.

9. Place the first part of the crumbled dough in the cake tin,

10. After this, spread the blueberry mixture over the dough.

11. Sprinkle the blueberry mixture with the second part of the dough.

12. Preheat the air fryer to 360 F.

13. Put the crumble in the air fryer and cook for 15 minutes.

14. When the dessert is cooked – let it chill briefly.

15. Enjoy!

Nutrition: calories 206, fat 12.4, fiber 0.8, carbs 22.5, protein 1.9

Conclusion

Thank you for making it through to the end of *The Essential Air Fryer Cookbook: Easy Recipes for Delicious Homemade Dishes, Low-Carb Breakfast, Lunch And Dinner For Rapid Weight Loss*, let's hope it was informative and able to provide you with all of the tools you need to achieve your goals whatever they may be.

The **Air Fryer** may take some time to get accustomed to. It takes time to determine new habits and become familiar with food replacement methods, including how to make low-cost food tasty and satisfying.

But if you keep up with it, it can become a replacement way of life that is natural and budget-friendly. It can also lead to some important health improvements, especially if you are suffering from any condition, keto diet proves to be helpful. And better health can mean fewer doctor visits and lower medical costs.

Finally, if you found this book useful in any way, a review is always appreciated!

Lightning Source UK Ltd.
Milton Keynes UK
UKHW020636010321
379583UK00012B/730

9 781801 947107